# Start with Art
# Still Life

© Aladdin Books Ltd 2000

Designed and produced by
Aladdin Books Ltd
28 Percy Street
London W1P 0LD

ISBN 0-7613-1166-1 (Lib. bdg.)
ISBN 0-7613-0842-3 (Trd. Pbk.)

First published in the United States
in 2000 by
Copper Beech Books,
an imprint of
The Millbrook Press
2 Old New Milford Road
Brookfield, Connecticut 06804

Project Editor
Sally Hewitt

Editor
Liz White

Designer
Flick Killerby

Illustrator
Catherine Ward - SGA

Picture Research
Brooks Krikler Research

Printed in Belgium

Original Design Concept
David West Children's Book Design

Cataloging-in-Publication data is on file at the Library of Congress

The project editor, Sally Hewitt, is an experienced teacher. She writes and edits books for children on a wide variety of subjects including art, music, science, and math.

The author, Sue Lacey, is an experienced teacher of art. She currently teaches primary school children in the south of England. In her spare time, she paints and sculpts.

**photocredits:** Abbreviations: t-top, m-middle, b-bottom, r-right, l-left,
Cover m & pages 3, 4t, 8, 12, 19, 20, 25, 29, 32 t, 32b: Roger Vlitos; cover b & pages 4b, 9, 11, 13, 24: AKG London;
17: AKG ©ADAGP, Paris &DACS, London 2000; 21: AKG © DACS 2000;23: AKG© Succession Picasso / DACS 2000; 27:
AKG ©ADAGP, Paris & DACS, London 2000; 18: Reproduced by permission of The Henry Moore Foundation; 28: AKG ©
Claes Oldenburg (Mitchell C. Shaheen, The Brett Mitchell Collection. Inc.) 31: Frank Spooner Pictures.

# Start with Art

# Still Life

## Sue Lacey

COPPER BEECH BOOKS
BROOKFIELD • CONNECTICUT

# INTRODUCTION

Artists work with many different tools and materials to make art. They also spend a great deal of time looking carefully at patterns, shapes, and colors in the world around them.

This book is about how artists see still life and objects. On every page you will find a work of art by a famous artist, featuring different objects.

It may be a painting, drawing, sculpture, or collage which will give you ideas and inspiration for the project.

You don't have to be a brilliant artist. Look at each piece of art, learn about the artist, and be creative.

# CONTENTS

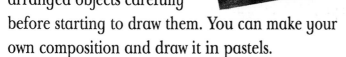

# WORKING LIKE AN ARTIST

It can help you in your work if you start by looking carefully and collecting ideas, just like an artist. Artists usually carry a sketchbook around with them all the time so they can get their ideas on paper right away.

**Words**
You can write some words to remind you of the shapes, colors, and patterns you see.

**Materials**
Try out different pencils, pens, paints, pastels, crayons, and materials to see what they do. Which would be the best for this work?

**Color**
When using color, mix all the colors you want first and try them out. It is amazing how many different colors you can make.

**Using a sketchbook** Before you start each project, this is the place to do your sketches. Try out your tools and materials, mix colors, and stick in some interesting papers and fabrics. You can then choose which you want to use.

**Be a magpie** Make a collection of things that are of interest to you like feathers, stones, or materials. Anything that catches your eye could be useful in your artwork.

**Art box** You can collect tools and materials together for your work and put them in a box. Sometimes you may need to go to an art store to buy exactly what you need. Often you can find things at home you can use. Ask for something for your art box for your birthday!

# Drawing objects

A still-life picture is made up of objects that are not alive. They can be studied easily because they do not move.

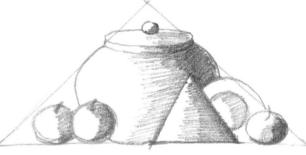

First the outline should be drawn and then the dark areas shaded, before finishing with lighter tones and highlights. This will give the object depth and make it look more realistic.

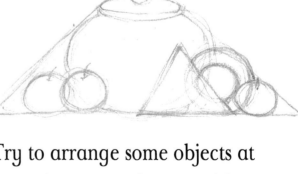

Try to arrange some objects at home into a good composition. Don't just put the objects in a line. Put some things at the front and some at the back. Look at what you have done and rearrange it until you are happy with it.

**WHAT YOU NEED**
Objects from
your Kitchen
Sketchbook • Pencil
Pastels

# COMPOSITION

Cézanne has put together lots of objects from a kitchen to make a still-life picture. If you collect some objects from your kitchen they can be drawn using oil pastels. Don't take months to draw it like Cézanne did!

### PROJECT: USING PASTELS

**Step 1.** Set up your still life, thinking about how you want the objects arranged. Make a light pencil sketch of your arrangement.

**Step 2.** Try blending and layering the oil pastels in your sketchbook. When you are confident, choose the medium shades of color and put them onto your sketch first. Remember to look carefully at the shapes you are drawing.

**Step 3.** After the shades of color, add the deep shadows, the shading, and the details last of all.

# GALLERY

## Still Life with Curtain, Jar, and Fruit Bowl 1893-94
## PAUL CÉZANNE (1839-1906)

**COLOR**
Look how many different colors Cézanne used just to cover one small area of wall.

**EYE**
Your eye is taken around the painting from the white cloth to see all the different objects.

**WHITE**
Although the cloth is white, what other colors have been used?

**LOOSE PAINT**
Paint has been used loosely to give an impression of objects, not every little detail.

The French artist Paul Cézanne painted such exciting and surprising pictures that many famous artists were inspired by his work. He was not an easy friend to have as he had a very bad temper. Despite this his work was always admired. Cézanne put dabs of paint next to each other to build up a whole picture. He called this method working with a "pistol loaded with paint."

# PAINTING FLOWERS

**WHAT YOU NEED**
Flowers • Sponge
Paper • Paint
Pastels • Hairspray
Paintbrushes
Colored Paper

Many artists including Odilon Redon have enjoyed painting flowers. Get some flowers from the garden or a florist and try out different printing and painting methods to make a colorful picture.

### PROJECT: MIXED MEDIA FLOWERS

**Step 1.** Look carefully at the flowers you have in front of you. You could paint each flower using a different method. Start with a piece of sponge to print the petals and leaves in different colors.

**Step 2.** Paintbrushes and fingers can be used to dab extra colors and shapes onto the flowers.

**Step 3.** When the paint has dried, add some pastel marks and small pieces of colored paper to give texture. You can spray it with hairspray to stop it from smudging.

# GALLERY

## Flowers in a Turquoise-Colored Vase c.1905
## ODILON REDON (1840-1916)

**BACKGROUND**
The colors of the flowers stand out against the background.

**VASE**
This vase catches your eye, too, with its bright color.

**MATERIALS**
Can you see brush strokes or other marks on the painting? What do you think Redon used to paint the flowers? Look at the texture of the leaves and the petals.

Odilon Redon was often sick as a child. He became very shy and liked to hide away from people as he grew up. He did not want to be an artist like the Impressionists. He used his imagination to make black and white prints and charcoal drawings. Later in his life he found happiness with his wife and friends and began to use color. He said, "Color contains joy."

# SCULPTING FRUIT

Gauguin has painted the fruit in this still life to look three-dimensional. You can make 3-D fruit by using paper and glue. The pieces of fruit could then be arranged into a still life.

## PROJECT: 3-D FRUIT

**Step 1.** Scrunch used newspaper into the shape of different fruit. Tape it together.

**Step 2.** Dip strips of newspaper into a mixture of glue and water. Wrap around the fruit. Leave it to dry.

**Step 3.** Paint each piece of fruit to look as real as possible.

**Step 4.** When the paint is dry, arrange your fruit into a still life.

# GALLERY

## Still Life with Profile of Laval 1886
## PAUL GAUGUIN (1848-1903)

**BRUSH**
Gauguin has used a large brush and loose strokes to paint his still life.

**COMPOSITION**
Laval looking at the fruit draws your eye in to look at it, too.

**OBJECTS**
What other objects can you see on the table that Laval is looking at?

**3-D EFFECT**
See how shadows, tones, and highlights make the fruit look three-dimensional.

Until the age of six, Paul Gauguin lived with his parents in Peru, South America. The colors, smells, and way of life stayed with him and he always longed to return. In 1883 he decided to become a painter and traveler. Later he lived abroad and painted using very bright colors.

# OBSERVATION

**WHAT YOU NEED**
Sketchbook
Selection of Pencils

Leonardo da Vinci was a keen artist and he also invented things. He would carefully observe the world and draw what he saw. You can also take your sketchbook out and draw the things around you.

## PROJECT: SKETCHING

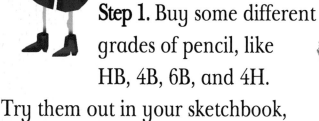

**Step 1.** Buy some different grades of pencil, like HB, 4B, 6B, and 4H. Try them out in your sketchbook, making as many different dark and light marks as you can.

**Step 2.** Look around your house or backyard for interesting objects to sketch. Make sure you look slowly and carefully before you start to draw. You can write notes about what you see, too.

**Step 3.** Now use these sketches to make a still-life drawing, using all the different pencils you have already tried out.

# GALLERY

## Sketches c.1508
## LEONARDO DA VINCI (1452-1519)

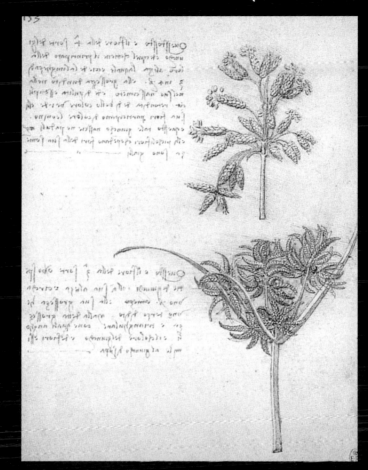

**WRITING BACKWARDS**
Da Vinci was left-handed. In the days of writing with pen and ink, this made things difficult – as you pushed the pen forward, your hand would trail over the ink. Leonardo had a better idea. He wrote backwards.

**DETAIL**
As there were no cameras to capture detail, Leonardo used his pencil to record plants and other objects.

**OBSERVATION**
Look how carefully he observed everything he wanted to paint.

Leonardo da Vinci was famous even in his own lifetime as a great artist and inventor. He was one of Italy's most gifted painters. He tried to make his paintings and drawings perfect. He made detailed studies of nature and the anatomy of the human body. He made sketches of airplanes, helicopters, and many other machines that were not even invented when he was alive.

# COLLAGE

Magritte did many paintings of everyday objects in places you wouldn't expect to see them. If you look for some pictures of places and objects in magazines, you can make a surrealist picture, too.

PROJECT: SURREALIST COLLAGE

**Step 2.** Put your chosen object into the frame so that you can still see some of the view around it.

**Step 1.** From a magazine, choose a picture of a room, landscape, or seascape. Glue it to a piece of cardboard. You can make a frame to go around it. Find a picture of an interesting object that will fill the cutout view, but that looks really strange. Try out a few first.

# GALLERY

The Listening Room 1958
## RENÉ MAGRITTE (1898-1967)

**SIZE**
Why do you think the apple is so large? Is it the only thing you look at in the picture?

**VIEWER**
What size does this picture make you feel?

**APPLE**
This apple looks so real you feel you could take a bite out of it.

**LISTENING**
Can you figure out why he called this picture "The Listening Room?"

By the age of 12, Magritte was going to painting classes. Later, he did a four-year art course in Brussels, Belgium, where he lived. He had many interesting ideas and said he wanted to express his thoughts in paint. He found the world a wonderful and mysterious place and, like Salvador Dali, became a surrealist painter. He often painted ordinary objects in strange places, such as a large apple in a small room.

# SCULPTURE

Henry Moore made sculptures using simple shapes. He often used clay to make a model of a large sculpture he was planning. Clay would be a good material for you to make a 3-D shape in the style of Henry Moore's work.

**WHAT YOU NEED**
Clay • Paint
Paintbrush

# GALLERY

## Oval with Points 1968-1970
## HENRY MOORE (1898-1986)

**VIEW**
Can you see how the shape makes a frame around the view through the center?

**SURFACE**
What material do you think Moore used? The surface catches the light.

**SIZE**
This shape is larger than life and fills a great deal of space.

**POINTS**
The two points almost touch and draw your eye to the center of the shape.

# PROJECT: SCULPTING IN CLAY

**Step 1.** Take a lump of clay and make it soft by rolling, shaping, and squeezing it. Mold it into the shape of a number eight.

**Step 2 .** Use your fingers to create two different-sized holes in the shape.

Growing up in Yorkshire, England, gave Henry Moore a great love of the countryside. He studied art in Leeds and London, but it wasn't until after World War II when Moore was in his forties, that he found fame. He continued to work until he was 88 years old. His main work was making enormous sculptures in bronze and stone that he placed in the countryside.

**Step 3 .** When the clay dries, you can paint it with bronze-colored paint or leave it clay-colored.

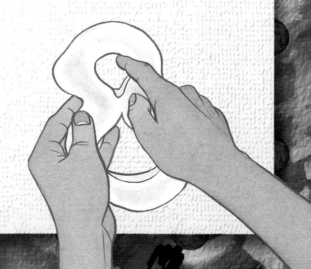

# MAKING A COLLECTION

WHAT YOU NEED
Shallow Box • Paint
Paintbrush
Cardboard
Scissors • Glue
Collection of
Interesting Things

Schwitters used tickets, stamps, postcards, advertisements, and other objects to make his works of art. If you collect things that you like, you can make an arrangement of them and they will remind you of good times.

## PROJECT: CONSTRUCTION

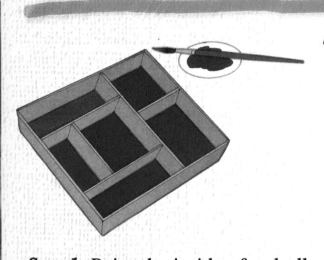

**Step 2.** When you have finished, glue the objects into the box. You could hang it on the wall.

**Step 1.** Paint the inside of a shallow box a bright color – for example, red. Divide the box up with cardboard strips, which you can also paint. Collect things that you like or that are special to you and arrange them in the sections of the box. Why not add your initials so your box is made personal?

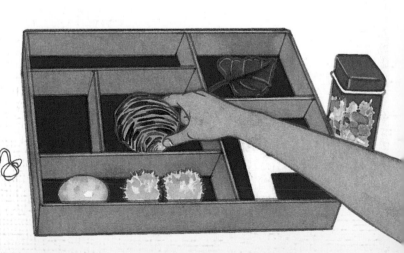

# GALLERY

## Merzbild P 1930
## KURT SCHWITTERS (1887-1948)

**MATERIALS**
How many different kinds of material can you see in this picture?

**ARRANGEMENT**
Do you like the way Schwitters has arranged his materials, or would you have done it differently?

**FEATURES**
One of the main features in this construction is the keyhole. The letter P is also very eye-catching.

Born in Germany, Kurt Schwitters later moved to Norway and then England where he stayed. His art is called abstract because he arranged objects at random without meaning. He collected different materials together and arranged them to make a picture or a construction. He gave this art the new name of Merz because no one had ever done art like it before.

# CUBISM

WHAT YOU NEED
Colored Paper
Black Felt Pen
Scissors • Glue
Pencils • Paint
Paintbrush

Picasso looked at the different planes and angles of an object and then painted it in a cubist style. If you draw an object then cut it up and rearrange it, you can make a cubist picture.

## PROJECT: CUBIST COLLAGE

**Step 1.** Use the objects in Picasso's picture or some you have chosen yourself. Draw them onto colored paper using a black felt pen.

**Step 2.** Draw and paint a background of a window onto a piece of cardboard. This will frame your image.

**Step 3.** Cut up the objects you have drawn using straight lines. Arrange them onto the background and glue them in place when you are happy with how it looks.

# GALLERY

## Guitar and Table in Front of a Window 1919
## PABLO PICASSO (1881-1973)

**WINDOW**
Picasso often used an open window as part of his painting to give it a sense of space.

**CUBISM**
Painting objects or people by using straight lines and geometric shapes is called Cubism.

**OBJECTS**
What other objects can you see in this picture?

**COLOR**
Picasso has chosen to use a range of colors for this picture. Are they warm or cool colors?

From an early age Pablo Picasso showed his talent at drawing. He spent his whole life making many different kinds of art, and produced more art than any other modern artist. Many people found his work hard to understand, but this did not stop him from fascinating the world with his unusual works of art.

# WORKING IN 3-D

Van Gogh lived a simple life, but his room looks attractive with its bright colors. You can bring Van Gogh's bedroom to life by making it in cardboard in three dimensions. When you have done that, you could also make a 3-D picture of your own room. Remember to clean it up first!

# GALLERY

## Vincent's Bedroom at Arles 1889
## VINCENT VAN GOGH 1853-1890

**BRUSHSTROKES**
These thick brush strokes look just like a wooden floor.

**SHADOWS**
There are no shadows in the room as the shutters are closed, keeping out the light.

# PROJECT: 3-D BEDROOM

**Step 1.** Cut the front off an old shoe box or other small box. Paint the walls and floor to look like Van Gogh's bedroom.

**Step 2.** Make a bed and chairs out of cardboard. Make sure they fit into the box. Paint them the same colors Van Gogh used.

Throughout his life Van Gogh was poor, often hungry, and ill. This is the bedroom in the house he shared with Paul Gauguin. The two artists worked together and they often argued as well, especially about who should clean the house. This painting shows how neat Van Gogh could be, and is a record of how he lived.

**Step 3.** When the furniture is dry, fold the bottom of the legs under. Arrange them in your room, and when you are happy with their positions, glue them to the floor of the box.

# ABSTRACT ART

WHAT YOU NEED
Paper • Pencil
Glue
Paintbrush
Paint
Printing Ink

Fernand Léger used abstract shapes in his work. He would paint them in bright colors. If you use bright colors, you will see how the different shapes that you paint stand out.

## PROJECT: ABSTRACT SHAPES

**Step 1.** Make a sketch of some shapes. You can use cylinders like Léger. Use a tube of glue to draw lines of glue over the pencil lines. Leave it until it is dry and really hard.

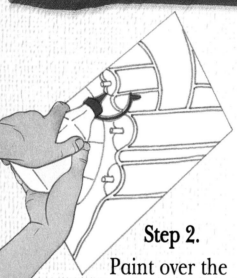

**Step 2.** Paint over the glue lines with dark paint or printing ink. Before the paint dries, press a piece of paper onto it.

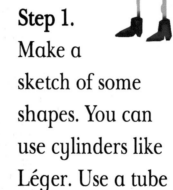

**Step 3.** Peel the paper off carefully and let it dry. When it has dried, paint bright, clear colors into the spaces.

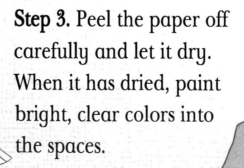

# GALLERY

## Cenpa 1953
## FERNAND LÉGER (1881-1955)

**COLOR**
Léger used clear, bright colors so that different parts of his painting stood out from each other.

**BLACK LINES**
Black lines around the shapes on Léger's painting make it look like a stained glass window.

**CYLINDERS**
The cylinder is often seen in Léger's work as many machines have this shape.

**MACHINES**
What kind of machine do you think has been painted here?

Fernand Léger was brought up on a farm in northern France. His father died when he was a small boy and as a young man he fought in World War I. Both events affected him a great deal. He often seemed angry, but he was kind underneath. The world was using more and more machines, and Léger used color, shape, and pattern to show the new "machine age" in which he lived.

**WHAT YOU NEED**
Cardboard • Glue
Scissors • Pencils
Interesting Fabric
Old Stockings
Needle and Thread
Old Material
Colored Cardboard

# USING MATERIAL

Oldenburg wanted to make art that was unusual. He took everyday objects and made them look strange. You don't have to be good at sewing to make soft sculptures like Oldenburg – glue will hold material together just as well as thread.

# GALLERY

## Soft Fur Good Humors 1963
## CLAES OLDENBURG (1929-)

**OPPOSITES**
Ice pops are usually icy and shiny. Here the material used is thick and fluffy.

**SIZE**
These ice pops are made much larger than real ones.

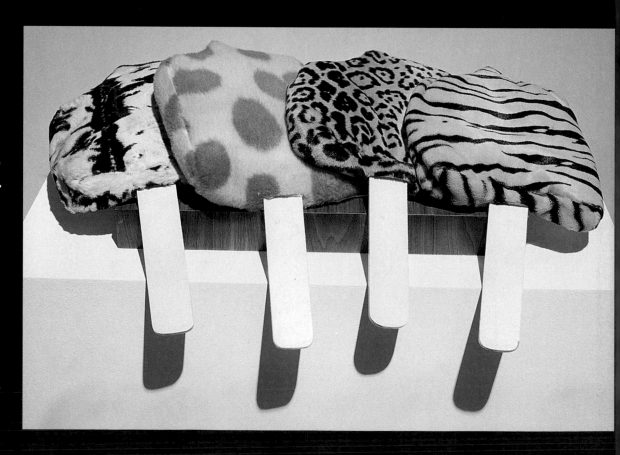

# PROJECT: SOFT SCULPTURE

**Step 1.** Cut out an ice pop shape from cardboard. Make it about 5 x 12 inches. Trace this shape twice onto a piece of interesting material. Sew or glue the edges of the two pieces together, leaving a hole at the bottom. Fill this with cut-up bits of material or old stockings.

Born in Norway, Claes Oldenburg also spent a great deal of his childhood in the United States. He graduated from Yale University and became a member of the Pop Art movement. He made everyday objects into large sculptures, which surprises people who see them because of their size. He often used soft fabrics for objects that are solid in real life.

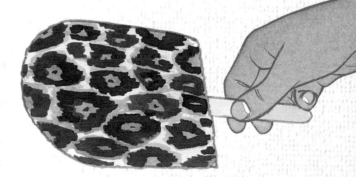

**Step 2.** Cut out a piece of colored cardboard for the stick and glue it into the base of the ice pop. You can make as many of these ice pops as you like in various colors and textures.

# PATTERN AND COLOR

WHAT YOU NEED
Paper Plate
Paints
Paintbrush

Aboriginal art uses patterns and warm colors to decorate all kinds of objects. This art uses color and pattern to great effect. You can decorate a plate in the same style.

## PROJECT: DECORATING A PLATE

**Step 1.** Take a paper plate and some bright natural colored paints.

**Step 2.** Start by painting the background of the plate. Divide it up into sections of bright colors. Let it dry.

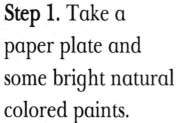

**Step 3.** When it is dry, you can add the pattern on top. Use black and white paint to stand out against the bright colors you have used. You could make your pattern a flower or another object that you might see in nature.

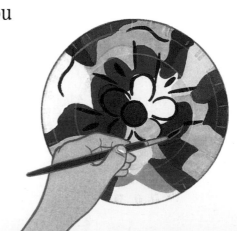

# GALLERY

## Aboriginal Artifact
## ABORIGINAL ART (PRESENT DAY)

**FABRICS**
Today Aboriginal designs are often used to decorate fabric that can be made into clothes.

**PATTERN**
This pattern is exactly the same as those that have been used by Aborigines for thousands of years.

**DOTS AND SPOTS**
The dot or circle was used a great deal in Aboriginal pattern making.

Aborigines have lived in Australia much longer than anyone else. From earliest times they used color to decorate their bodies, rocks, wooden and clay pots, spears, boomerangs, and shields. Crushed rocks and flowers were used as paints, while feathers and chewed bark served as brushes. Today in some parts of Australia, this same style is used to decorate objects used in everyday life.

# GLOSSARY

**ABSTRACT ART** A work of art that is not an exact copy. Shape, color, and pattern are used to give a feel of the subject.

**CHARCOAL** Slightly burned twigs or sticks that turn black and are used by artists for drawing.

**CONSTRUCTION** Materials fitted together to make a work of art.

**CUBISM** An art movement using distorted shapes to show objects from more than one angle.

**FABRIC** Material or cloth made by weaving.

**IMPRESSIONISTS** A group of French artists who painted an impression of what they were looking at.

**OBJECT** Something that is not alive but can be seen or touched.

**OBSERVATION** Looking closely at something so that a more accurate work of art can be made.

**POP ART** Art made by using popular pictures or ideas.

**PRINT** A picture made by pressing paper onto a marked surface.

**SCULPTURE** An object made from hard or soft materials that can be looked at from all sides.

**STILL LIFE** Lifeless objects grouped together to make a picture.

**SURFACE** The outside of something that you can see and feel.

**SURREALISM** A way of putting unlikely objects together into a strange landscape to make an unreal or dream-like work of art.

**THREE-DIMENSIONAL** An object or work of art is three-dimensional if you can walk around and look at it from all sides.

# INDEX